DPT

W9-BFH-345

VISIT US AT
www.abdopublishing.com

Published by ABDO Publishing Company, 8000 West 78th Street, Edina, Minnesota 55439.

Copyright © 2009 by Abdo Consulting Group, Inc. International copyrights reserved in all countries. No part of this book may be reproduced in any form without written permission from the publisher. Buddy Books™ is a trademark and logo of ABDO Publishing Company.

Printed in the United States.

Coordinating Series Editor: Rochelle Baltzer
Editor: Sarah Tieck
Contributing Editor: Marcia Zappa
Graphic Design: Deborah Coldiron
Cover Photograph: *iStockPhoto*: Brian McClister, Michal Rozanski, Mike Sonnenberg
Interior Photographs/Illustrations: *iStockPhoto*: Carlos Alvarez (p. 19), Jani Bryson (pp. 13, 24, 29), Jeff Chiasson (p. 19), Merrill Dyck (p. 18), Walter Fumagalli (p. 13), David T. Gomez (p. 9), Eileen Hart (p. 10), Chris Hepburn (p. 15), David Hernandez (p. 30), Graham Heywood (p. 29), Stephanie Howard (p. 9), iStockPhoto (pp. 7, 9, 13, 17, 25, 30), Bonnie Jacobs (p. 26), Sebastian Kaulitzki (p. 15), Roman Kobzarev (p. 25), Bela Tibor Kozma (p. 17), Cat London (p. 28), Jason Lugo (p. 21), Ivan Mateev (p. 9), Cliff Parnell (p. 21), Holly Sisson (p. 23), Mike Sonnenberg (pp. 9, 14), Igor Terekhov (p. 11), Anatoly Tiplyashin (p. 29), Suzanne Tucker (p. 16); *Peter Arnold, Inc.:* Howard Sochurek/The Medical File (p. 27); *Photos.com:* Jupiter Images (pp. 4, 19, 22).

Library of Congress Cataloging-in-Publication Data

Murray, Julie, 1969-
 The body / Julie Murray.
    p. cm. -- (That's gross! A look at science)
  ISBN 978-1-60453-554-9
 1. Body, Human--Juvenile literature. 2. Human anatomy--Juvenile literature. 3. Gastrointestinal gas--Juvenile literature. 4. Excretion--Juvenile literature. 5. Body fluids--Juvenile literature. I. Title.
  QM27.M79 2009
  612--dc22
                          2008036382

Contents

Exploring the Body

Your body is amazing. It breathes. It grows. It heals. Look a little closer. You'll see that behind all that cool stuff is a lot of yuck. Some of it is natural. Some of it is unhealthy. Let's explore!

Ever hear gurgling in your belly? Food travels from your mouth to your stomach. From there, it moves through your intestines before it is pooped out.

Bacteria can make your feet and armpits stink!

Gas escapes through your mouth and rear end.

5

What's That Smell?

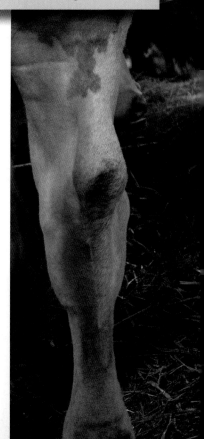

Animals pass gas, too. In fact, cows fart so much that some scientists say it might be adding to greenhouse gases. Many scientists believe these gases are what cause a rise in Earth's temperatures. This is called global warming.

It's been called tooting, cutting the cheese, passing gas, and farting. Call it what you want, but every human does it. As much as 14 times in a day! This lets out about 17 fluid ounces (500 mL) of stinky gas. Eeeeww!

P. U.!

Farts can travel fast.
They can come out
at a speed of ten feet per
second (3 m/s)!

The scientific name for farting is flatulence (FLA-chuh-luhns). Farts happen because gas builds up during **digestion** or when people swallow air. This trapped gas sometimes escapes through your rear end.

Even though it smells gross, farting is good. It means your body's bowel system is in healthy working order!

Certain foods create super stinky gas as they are digested. These foods include cheese, eggs, cabbage, and beans.

Number Two

Your body uses most of the food that enters your mouth. Food that can't be used becomes poop. Every body is different and every person eats different things. So, there are many kinds of poop.

Number two comes in brown, green, tan, and even black. It can be smooth, soft, or sticky. Sometimes it is dry or chunky. Usually it is pretty smelly.

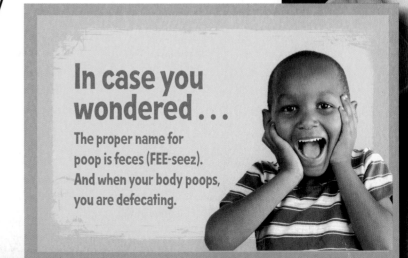

In case you wondered...

The proper name for poop is feces (FEE-seez). And when your body poops, you are defecating.

Some bathrooms have bidets (bih-DAYS). A bidet is a special sink that cleans your bottom after you use the toilet. In Europe, some people use bidets instead of toilet paper.

11

Poop is also called a bowel movement. After you eat, your stomach **digests** the food. It passes the digested food into the bowels. The small intestine removes the **nutrients** (NOO-tree-uhnts) from the waste. Then, the large intestine helps push out the solid waste.

When you eat corn, you might see it in your poop later. Corn is hard for the digestive system to break down.

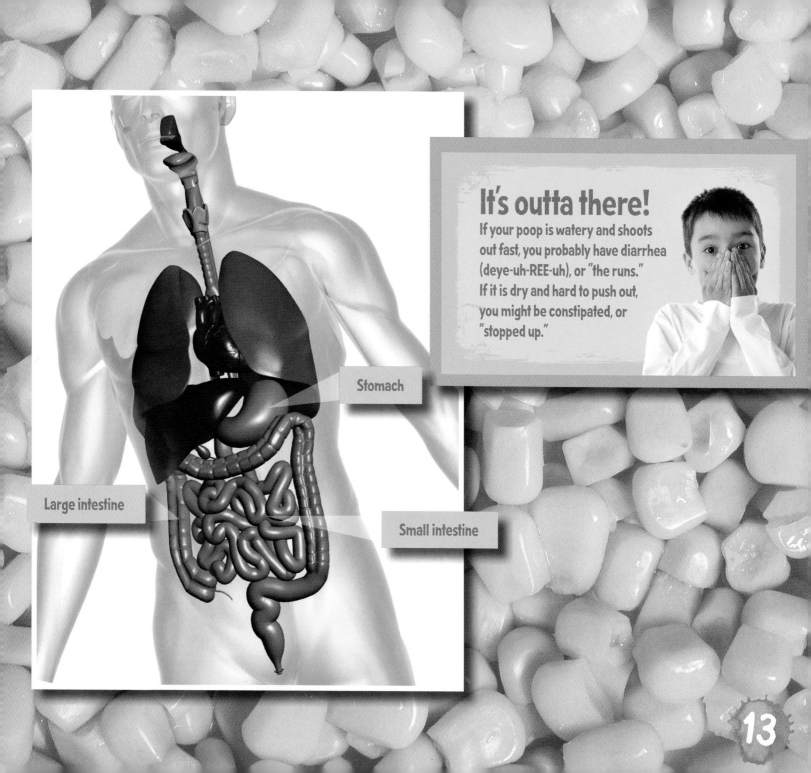

Stomach

Large intestine

Small intestine

It's outta there!

If your poop is watery and shoots out fast, you probably have diarrhea (deye-uh-REE-uh), or "the runs." If it is dry and hard to push out, you might be constipated, or "stopped up."

When You've Gotta Go . . .

There's no mistaking the feeling of having to pee. The action of peeing is called urinating (YUHR-uh-nayt-ihng). Doing this helps clean out the body to keep it healthy.

Pee changes based on water levels and what a person has eaten. Sometimes, pee is dark yellow and stinky. Other times, it is clear and doesn't smell.

Washing your hands after using the bathroom is important. Doing this protects you from unseen germs found in poop and pee that can make you sick.

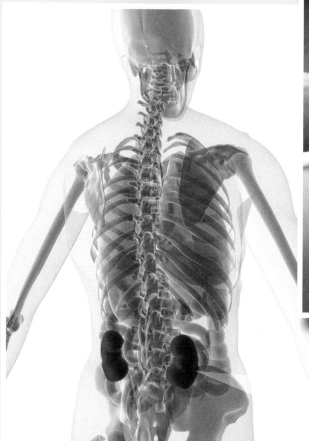

The official name for pee is urine. Urine is made by the kidneys. Most people have two kidneys.

Scab-enger Hunt

Have you ever fallen down and cut your knee? What happened? Did your blood dry into a dark, crusty spot? This is called a scab.

Inside a cut, gooey blood creates a **clot** (KLAHT), which dries into a scab. This covers the wound to help your skin heal. It is like a natural bandage.

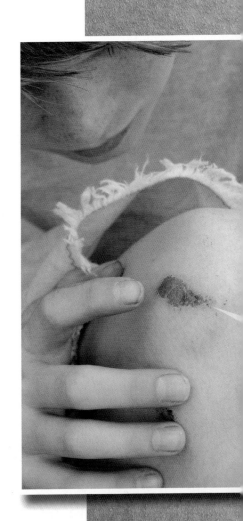

After you have a scab for a couple of weeks, the skin heals itself. Then, the scab falls off. You might get a scar where the scab was.

17

Gooey Ears

Earwax looks like a glob of jelly. It can be gray, yellow, orange, or brown. Your ear makes this soft, sticky stuff.

Earwax helps keep the ear moist, clean, and healthy. It catches dirt and **bacteria** (bak-TIHR-ee-uh). This keeps your body safe. And, earwax helps fight **infection** (ihn-FEHK-shuhn). That is some cool goo!

Many people use cotton swabs to clean their ears. But, most doctors say this can push earwax farther into the ear. It can also hurt the eardrums, which help people hear.

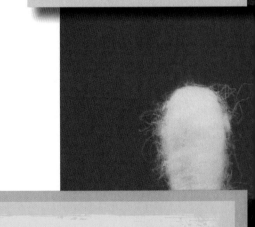

Huh?

Whales have earwax too. Some types of whales add a new layer every year. So, scientists use this to find out the whale's age.

18

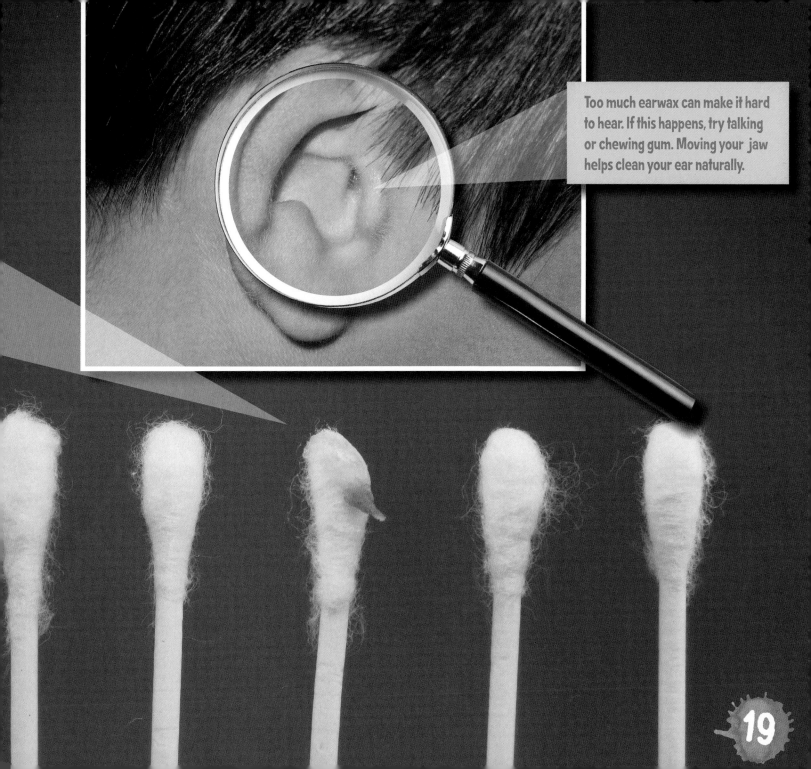

Too much earwax can make it hard to hear. If this happens, try talking or chewing gum. Moving your jaw helps clean your ear naturally.

Stinky Parts

Have you ever been sticky, drippy, and covered in sweat? This happens when you perspire, or let out sweat.

Perspiration is good! **Glands** in your skin create sweat. This helps your body cool off when it is too hot.

Sweat is mostly water. The smell of sweaty armpits and feet is actually **bacteria** living on your skin. Bacteria eat sweat. When they **digest** it, they produce stinky waste.

20

The average person has more than 2 million sweat glands!

Yuck!

Armpit sweat can leave a yucky yellow circle on your shirt's underarms.

21

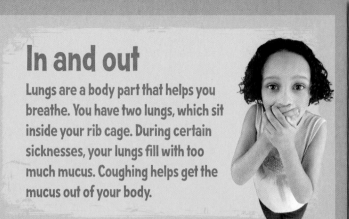

Snot Rockets

Did you say your nose is running? Well, you better catch it! All kidding aside, runny noses are no laughing matter.

Snot is actually called **mucus** (MYOO-kuhs). Mucus guards your lungs from sickness. Sticky mucus catches dirt and **germs** (JUHRMS) that your lungs breathe in with air. Boogers are made of dried snot and the dirt and germs it has collected.

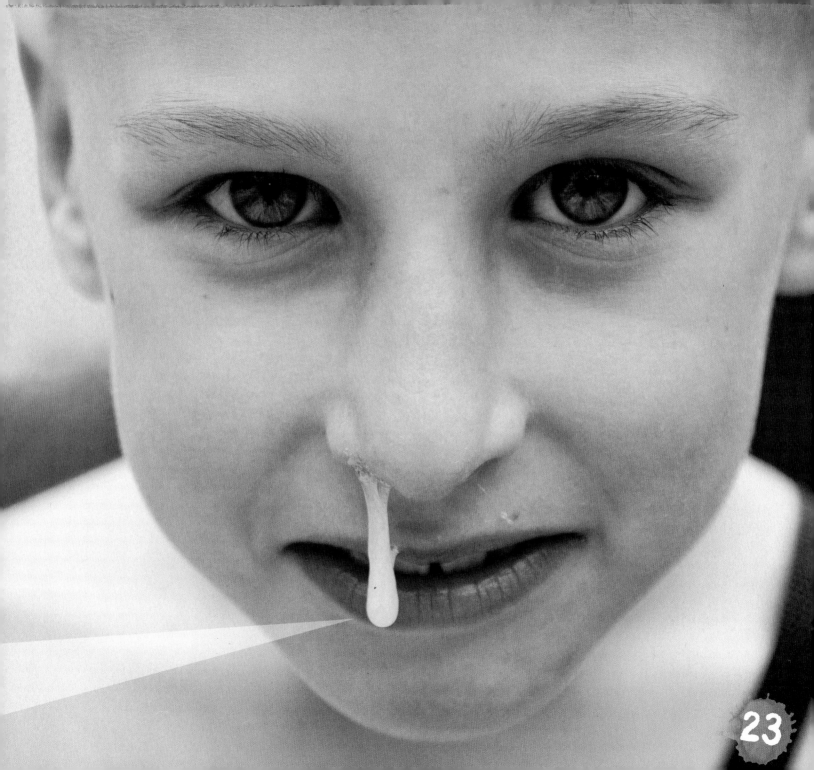

23

Belch-o-Rama

Have you ever experienced an eructation (ih-ruhk-TAY-shuhn)? Most people do this daily. Eructations are otherwise known as burps or belches.

When people burp, their bodies are letting out gas. While eating and drinking, people swallow gas they don't need. Burping allows the gas to escape.

Ever notice that you burp after drinking soda? A gas called carbon dioxide helps make soda fizzy. When you drink soda, the bubbles carry this gas into your stomach. Your body burps to remove this unneeded gas.

25

Barf Bag

Puking, ralphing, hurling, and barfing are all words to describe vomiting. When you vomit, you really do lose your lunch.

Vomit consists of food, stomach juices, and spit. This liquid combination travels fast from your stomach through your throat. Then, it bursts out of your mouth. Barfing leaves a stinky, gooey mess.

Ick!
The taste and color of puke depends on what you eat or drink. So, drinking red fruit juice could make your puke red and slightly sweet.

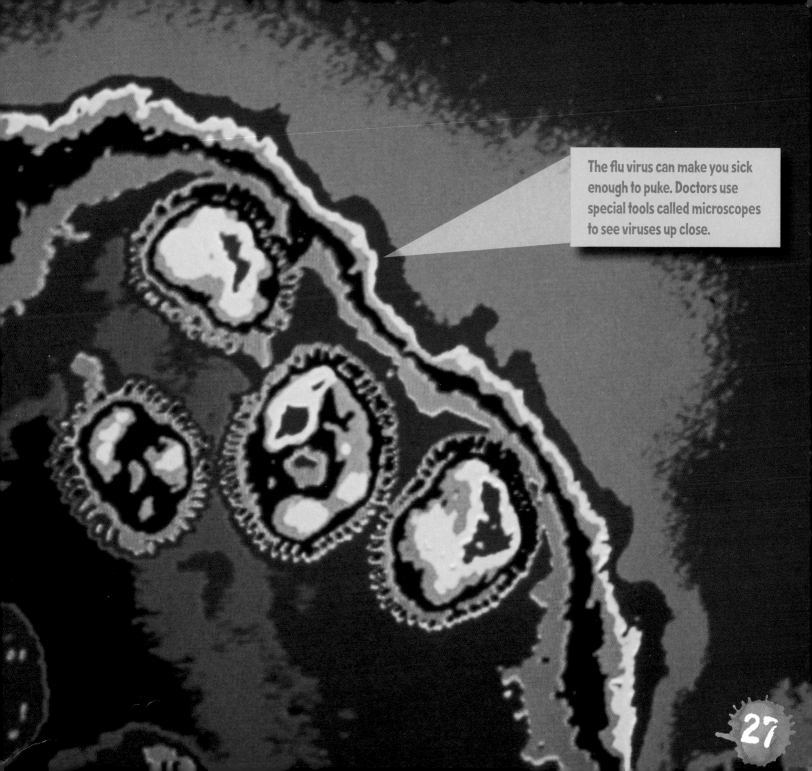

The flu virus can make you sick enough to puke. Doctors use special tools called microscopes to see viruses up close.

27

That WAS Gross!

Between stinky farts, gooey puke, and oozing scabs, your body does some very yucky things!

Now that you know about all the grossness, take a closer look. Many gross things are just a part of life and no big deal. Others can be prevented. Do what you can to live in a healthy way!

Some people put deodorant or antiperspirant on their armpits. This helps their sweaty pits smell better. Other people just wash with soap and water.

It's okay to fart! But if you fart near someone else, be sure to say, "excuse me."

Babies take in lots of extra air when they eat. That's why adults burp them after they are fed. Gassy babies often cry because their stomachs hurt.

Eeeeww! What is THAT?

Answer on page 32.

30

Important Words

bacteria tiny one-celled organisms that can only be seen through a microscope. Some are germs.

clot a thick clump of blood.

digest to break down food into parts small enough for the body to use.

germs harmful organisms that can make people sick.

gland a body part that makes things the body needs. For example, sweat glands let out sweat to cool the skin.

infection the causing of an unhealthy condition by something harmful, such as bacteria.

mucus thick, slippery, protective fluid from the body.

nutrient something found in food that living beings take in for growth and development.

Web Sites

To learn more about gross stuff, visit ABDO Publishing Company online. Web sites about gross stuff are featured on our Book Links page. These links are routinely monitored and updated to provide the most current information available.

www.abdopublishing.com

31

Index

"Eeeeww! What is THAT?" answer: a scar.